FOCUS ON

AZTECS AND INCAS

Chloë Sayer

SHOOTING STAR PRESS

This edition produced in **1995** for
Shooting Star Press Inc
230 Fifth Avenue
Suite 1212
New York, NY 10001

© Aladdin Books Ltd 1995

Designed and produced by
Aladdin Books Ltd
28 Percy Street
London W1P 0LD

*First published in the
United States in 1995 by*
Shooting Star Press Inc

ISBN 1-57335-324-8

Printed in Belgium

Editor	Jon Richards
Design	David West Children's Book Design
Designer	Ed Simkins
Series Director	Bibby Whittaker
Illustrator	Dave Burroughs
Picture research	Brooks Krikler Research

*The author, Chloë Sayer, has written
numerous books on Mexico. She has worked
as a television consultant on documentaries
about Mexico, Peru, and Spain for British
television, and has made ethnographic
collections for the British Museum in Mexico
and Belize.*

INTRODUCTION

The Aztecs and the Incas created two of the greatest planned societies the world has known. Both civilizations dominated huge areas and ruled over numerous peoples. The Aztecs and their allies ruled most of present-day Mexico. At its height, the Inca empire covered Peru, Ecuador, Bolivia, and neighboring areas of Chile and Argentina. Throughout these regions lie the dazzling remains of what were two of the most powerful empires in the world. This book aims to give an insight into Aztec and Inca achievements. It includes information about language and literature, science and math, history, geography, and the arts. The key below shows how the subjects are divided up.

Geography

The symbol of the planet Earth is used where geographical facts are used. These sections look at the migration of early hunters across the Bering Strait, and the habitats of Mexico and Peru.

Language and Literature

An open book is the sign for activities which involve language. These sections discuss the manuscripts of the Aztecs, and storytelling among the Incas. They also explore the legend of El Dorado.

Science and Math

The microscope symbol is used where a science or math subject is included. These sections study Aztec foodstuffs and weaponry, also the Inca calendar, the quipu and animal husbandry.

History

The sign of the scroll and hourglass indicates that historical facts are included. Sections explore the rise and fall of pre-Aztec and pre-Inca civilizations. They also discuss the arrival from Spain of Cortés and Pizarro.

Social History

The symbol of the family shows where information about social history is included. These sections aim to provide an insight into the everyday lives of Aztecs and Incas, and the social structure of Aztec and Inca cities.

Arts, Crafts, and Music

The symbol showing a sheet of music and art tools indicates art, crafts or musical information. Sections discuss gold and feather working, painting, weaving, and influences upon twentieth-century artists, such as Diego Rivera.

CONTENTS

EARLY AMERICA

The first inhabitants of the Americas were migrants from eastern Asia who gathered wild plant foods, wore skins, and used sharp points made from flaked stone to hunt mammoths, mastodons, antelopes, horses, and other animals. Later cultures made simple nets, baskets, mats, and rope. They also began to rely more on the cultivation of several plants, such as maize. Over long periods of time separate cultures, such as the Olmecs and Nazca, developed in North and South America, without any proven influence from the outside world until the arrival of the Europeans some 500 years ago.

Before the Aztecs
In Mexico the first major civilization was that of the Olmecs, who inhabited the tropical lowlands of the Gulf Coast between 1200 and 600 B.C. The era between A.D. 300 and 900 was marked by great advances in architecture and other arts. During the 10th and 11th centuries, much of central Mexico was dominated by the warlike Toltecs. In the southeast, the Zapotecs and later the Mixtecs forged their own distinctive cultures. The Maya excelled as architects, painters, and sculptors.

Pre-Aztec civilizations

NORTH AMERICA

Totonacs
Toltecs
Olmecs
Maya
Mixtecs
Copán

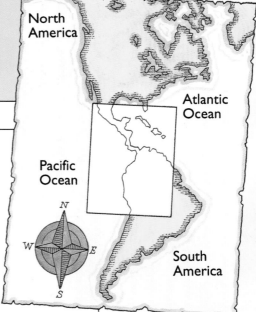

North America

Atlantic Ocean

Pacific Ocean

South America

N
W E
S

The city of Copán
After the Ice Age, climatic changes and over-hunting killed off several American animal species, including the horse and the mammoth. Some 7,000 years ago, hunting and gathering societies learned how to cultivate maize crops. This allowed people to live in large, settled communities. Copán, in what is now Honduras, was one of many cities built by the ancient Maya. The city was a complex of many stone temples, palaces, and recreational areas.

Peoples of South America

The Incas were the last in a long line of important civilizations in South America. These included the Vicús, the Cajamarca, the Nazca, the Tiahuanaco, the Mochica, and later the Chimú. Chan Chan, the Chimú capital (right), was built from sun-dried mud-bricks and, at its peak, sheltered some 50,000 people.

Olmec stone head

SOUTH AMERICA

Mochica pottery

Pre-Inca civilizations

Vicús
Mochica
Cajamarca
Recuay
Lima
Huarpa
Waru
Nazca
Tiahuanaco
Atacameño

The land bridge

During the Great Ice Age, vast quantities of water were locked up in glaciers and ice sheets across the globe. Low sea levels exposed a wide platform of land across the Bering Strait, between Siberia and the western coast of Alaska. Nomadic tribes from Asia crossed this bridge (below), between 30,000 and 8,000 B.C. From here they fanned out across North, Central, and South America. These early peoples lived by hunting herds of grazing animals such as mammoths, horses, and giant bison. They also gathered from the huge variety of plants that thrived on the continent.

Land bridge
Siberia
Alaska

THE RISE OF THE AZTECS

The beginnings of the Aztec nation were humble and obscure. Yet, in the space of just a few hundred years, it rose to rule over most of Mexico. The Aztecs, who called themselves the Mexica or Tenochca, arrived in the Valley of Mexico in the thirteenth century after a long migration. They were the last of many tribes to settle in this area, and found the best land already occupied. The shores of Lake Texcoco proved a miserable home for the Aztecs, who were forced to serve as vassals to the more powerful tribes.

Aztec beginnings

History and myth suggest that the Aztecs came originally from Aztlán, meaning "Place of Herons," in the west of Mexico. When representing their early history in manuscripts, the Aztecs used footprints to indicate their migration route (right). In 1325, the Aztecs took refuge on a previously uninhabited and marshy island near the western edge of Lake Texcoco in the Valley of Mexico. They founded their home where they saw the sign that their gods had promised them; an eagle on a prickly pear. Today, this symbol appears in the middle of the Mexican flag (top).

The Toltec influence

The warlike Toltecs dominated most of central Mexico between A.D. 900 and 1170. Tula, the Toltec capital, was just north of the Valley of Mexico. Toltec architecture was full of military images, and the roof of the main temple at Tula was supported by stone columns carved into warriors and plumed serpents (right). The Aztecs greatly admired the Toltecs. They called the Toltec period a golden age, and honored the memory of Tula as a center of power and civilization.

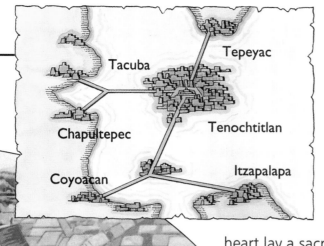

The glorious city

From a cluster of reed and grass huts, Tenochtitlan grew into one of the largest cities in the world. It was linked to the mainland by three causeways and ringed by several small· towns, such as Tepeyac and Itzapalapa (top left). Wooden drawbridges controlled access to the island. At the city's heart lay a sacred precinct dominated by the twin shrines (left) dedicated to Huitzilopochtli (god of war and the sun) and Tlaloc (god of rain and green growth). In 1519, Tenochtitlan held nearly 300,000 inhabitants. In comparison, Toledo, the royal capital of Spain, had 18,000.

Living at the water's edge

Since Tenochtitlan was situated on a lake, its streets were, in fact, a network of canals. Families who settled along these canals, or at the lake's edge, traveled around in boats. Their homes tended to be one-storey dwellings, with walls of sticks or adobe (dried mud bricks), and thatched roofs.

Chinampas and land reclamation

The Aztecs made the most of their swampy and inhospitable environment by digging ditches to reclaim large areas of land from the lake, and canals, some of which can still be seen (below). They also built mounds covered with mud and grass, and chinampas. These were "rafts" of wickerwork and branches, floating in the lake. On these the Aztecs grew all of their plant foods.

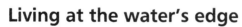

THE AZTEC EMPIRE

Just as Tenochtitlan grew from small town to large city, so the Aztec empire expanded through war and diplomacy. In 1428, after a decisive victory, the Triple Alliance was formed between Tenochtitlan and the neighboring towns of Texcoco and Tacuba. During the reign of Moctezuma I (1440-68), Aztec soldiers pushed eastward and southward. Under his successor, Axayacatl (1468-81), the domination of Tenochtitlan was extended westward and further south toward the coast of the Pacific Ocean.

Gulf of Mexico

Aztec empire

Tenochtitlan

Pacific Ocean

Warfare
War was basic to the Aztec way of life. As a warrior captured more prisoners, he had the right to wear a more elaborate costume.

War and empire
War was regarded as the most glorious of all activities. It provided captives for sacrifice and extended the boundaries of Aztec empire. By the time of the Spanish Conquest in 1519, the Aztecs and their allies ruled most of present day Mexico, from the desert zone in the north, to Oaxaca on the Pacific coast (above). This vast territory was not organized as a unified empire, but into subject states. These were required to pay tribute to the ruling Aztecs. From the hot lands of the Gulf coast came peppers, cloth, jade, and turquoise, and from the south-east came balls of rubber, parrot feathers, skins, cocoa, and amber. Cooler provinces provided maize and live eagles.

Jaguar Knights
Jaguar Knights (above) were seen as the soldiers of the night sky. They looked out through the open jaws of jaguar-shaped helmets, and wore jaguar skins.

Eagle Knights

In Aztec society a man's status depended on his success as a warrior. Consistently successful warriors could enter an order like the Knights of the Eagle (below). They were the soldiers of the Sun, and wore eagle-head helmets, often with tufts of feathers. Close-fitting body armor of quilted cotton, soaked in brine, served as protection against clubs and missiles.

Weaponry

The Aztec warrior was trained to use a range of weapons. These included bows and arrows, spears, and wooden sword-clubs edged with blades of obsidian, a hard volcanic glass. Warriors used the spearthrower, or *atlatl*, to propel barbed darts or javelins (below). It could also be used for hunting animals and large fish.

Tribute

The great imperial city of Tenochtitlan was too large to be self-sufficient, and relied on regular payments of tribute by conquered towns. Lists were recorded in pictorial form of what each town was required to provide. Towns, represented here by pictures in the left-hand column, were compelled to deliver warriors' costumes, shields, cotton mantles, and many other items (left).

The War of Flowers

The Aztecs believed themselves obliged to offer their gods a neverending supply of sacrificial victims. Not far from Tenochtitlan lay the independent state of Tlaxcala. Aztec warriors were able to secure captives (right) for sacrifice by engaging in military campaigns against the Tlaxcalans. These highly-organized ritual combats were known as the *xochiyaoyotl*, or "flowery war."

AZTEC RELIGION

The Aztecs regarded themselves as "the people of the sun." Huitzilopochtli (hummingbird-on-the-left) was the god of war and the sun, and was the most important god to the Aztecs. They did, however, worship many other gods, including Tezcatlipoca (smoking mirror), and Quetzalcoatl (plumed serpent). The Aztecs believed it was essential to offer the gods a stream of human sacrifices, in order to regenerate the cosmos and help the sun on its daily journey across the sky.

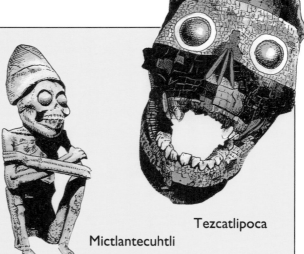

The gods

Aztec deities were depicted in gold, jade, stone, clay, wood, and other materials. Tezcatlipoca's emblem was an obsidian mirror. His mask was made from a human skull decorated with a mosaic of turquoise, lignite, and shell. Quetzalcoatl was the plumed serpent god. His turquoise mosaic mask (top) has a pair of serpents entwined around the eyes, nose, and mouth. Mictlantecuhtli was Lord of the Region of Death. This sandstone carving (right) shows him with a skull mask.

Mictlantecuhtli

Tezcatlipoca

Human sacrifice

Human sacrifice was practiced by the Aztecs on a huge scale. Victims, regarded as the gods' messengers, were thrown on the sacrificial stone and their hearts cut out (right). Sacrificial knives (left) were highly decorated, inlaid with turquoise, jade, and shell.

Temples

The Aztec city was dominated by the great double temple of Huitzilopochtli and Tlaloc (right). To mark its inauguration in 1487, 20,000 captive warriors were sacrificed. This huge monument, dedicated to warfare and agriculture, was built in seven stages. Aztec builders increased the size of the massive pyramid by building each new construction onto earlier ones.

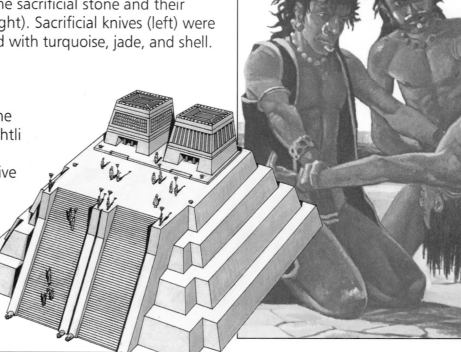

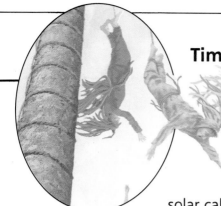

Time and the cosmos

The Aztec Calendar Stone (right) commemorates the five world-creations. To count time, the Aztecs used a solar calendar of 365 days and a sacred calendar of 260 days. The combination of these led to cycles of 52 years. Each year had many festivals, such as the Flying Dance, which saw five men climb a pole. While one played music, four "flew" to the ground, suspended on ropes (left).

Pyramids

Egyptian pyramids were monumental tombs. Built of stone with a rubble core, they covered or contained a burial chamber, and were thought to guarantee the well-being of kings in the afterlife. Early pyramids had stepped sides (bottom), but later ones were given straight sides to represent the sun's rays. Although they knew nothing of Egyptian pyramids, the Maya of ancienct Mexico and the Aztecs after them built very similar structures. These stepped pyramids had temples at the summit, unlike Egyptian pyramids and were rarely used as tombs (right).

AZTEC SOCIETY

Tenochtitlan was divided into four sections, and sub-divided into wards, known as *calpulli*, each with its own temple and an elected head. The whole of Aztec society operated according to strict laws. At the summit was the emperor. Below him were warriors, state officials, and priests who had their own hierarchies. Merchants and craftworkers formed classes apart. Below them came the majority of citizens. Slaves belonged to the lowest order: some were prisoners of war, while others had been condemned to slavery as a punishment.

Everyday life

Life for the common people was strictly regulated; even their clothing was governed by laws. Women wore a wrap-around skirt and a tunic-like blouse. Men wore a loincloth with a cape that stopped above the knee. The punishment was death if the cape reached the ankles. Parents trained their children with severity. Boys were taught how to fish, cultivate land, and manage boats. Later on they attended school. Girls, meanwhile, were taught how to spin thread, weave clothing, and prepare food (right).

Food

The Aztecs ate many foods that are now commonplace on our tables (below). Maize provided ground-maize pancakes, known today as *tortillas*, and cakes of dough. Other plant foods included beans, squash, chilli peppers, avocado pears, sweet potatoes, tomatoes, and cocoa. Animals eaten included turkey.

Markets

Exotic merchandise and local produce were sold in the great marketplace of the Aztec capital. Barter, offering other goods or services, was the usual means of buying things, but cocoa beans and lengths of cloth could serve as currency. Gold dust was also used to pay, and was carried in hollowed out feather quills. Each product was gathered in its own special place. There were vendors of foodstuffs, obsidian blades, ornaments of gold and jade, feathers, pottery, and textiles (right).

The emperor

At the head of the Aztec hierarchy was the emperor. Theoretically appointed by the gods, emperors were in reality elected by a group of high-ranking officials, priests and warriors. Aztec emperors lived in splendor, with palaces and gardens in different places. They would reward successful warriors with status-enhancing gifts (left), including jewels and feather ornaments. The emperor was carried around in a litter by four chiefs (main picture).

Merchants and trade

The state was dependent not just on tribute but also on trade. Aztec merchants were a powerful and privileged class. Setting out on missions lasting months, even years, they led their bands of porters along a network of trade routes to bring back luxury goods to the Aztec capital (below). They even acted as spies, traveling in disguise through enemy territory. Although many merchants grew rich, they had to conceal their wealth in public, by law. They lived together in the same city wards, and married among themselves.

THE ARTS

Aztec men and women wove their own clothes and made their own pots. There were, in addition, professional craftworkers who were divided into guilds and lived in specially designated areas within the city. Goldsmiths, feather-workers, and jewelers were known as "Toltecs" to show their link with the golden age of the past. Painters were also held in high esteem, some decorating monuments with brightly colored wall-paintings, while others worked as scribes, creating manuscripts, known as *codices*.

Gold!

The art of gold-working was brought to Tenochtitlan by Mixtec craftsmen from Oaxaca. Gold was panned and collected as nuggets from riverbeds, then shaped into ornaments. These included masks (top), animals, earrings, chest ornaments, and armbands (right). After the conquest, most of these treasures were melted down by the Spanish, but a few pieces remain to show the skill of their creators.

Language and song

The Aztecs spoke Nahuatl. By 1519, this expressive language had become the dominant tongue throughout central Mexico. In the codices, characters were often shown with a blue speech-scroll to show authority (right). Aztec songs were written by princes and priests.

Codices

In Aztec Mexico, codices were painted on folded strips of deerskin, bark paper, or even agave paper (right). They showed Aztec astrology, history, prophesy, and tribute lists, in picture form. Gods, rulers, priests, and warriors were shown in profile.

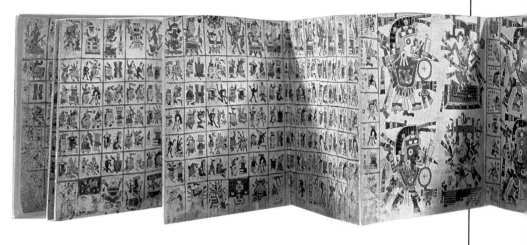

Feather-working

Among the most skilled of all the artisans were the *amanteca*, or feather-workers, who inhabited a city ward called Amantla. Using precious plumes sent to the capital as tribute, they fashioned the headdresses and shields used by high-ranking warriors (above). The amanteca fixed feathers to a reed framework by tying each one with cotton thread. They also pasted them onto cloth or paper to form a dazzling mosaic. They made an array of clothes and ornaments, including headdresses (main picture). Some (far left) were made from the plumes of the quetzal bird, then trimmed with gold, silver, and gemstones.

Hieroglyphics

The ancient Egyptians wrote on papyrus paper and carved inscriptions on stone (below), and, like the Aztecs, used a form of picture writing, called hieroglyphics. This system used a combination of signs for ideas and sounds. In 1519, the Aztec system of writing used symbols that conveyed whole ideas, or entire words. For instance, scribes would use footprints to show travel.

Yet the Aztecs were moving toward a form of writing that represented individual sounds as well. To convey Tenochtitlan, scribes drew a stone (tena) from which sprouted a nopal cactus (nochtli).

THE RISE OF THE INCAS

Like the Aztecs, the Incas arrived late on the historical scene. The Inca dynasty was founded around A.D. 1200 by Manco Capac at Cuzco in the Peruvian Andes. For the next 200 years, he and his descendants engaged in local wars. The first emperor to dramatically extend the territories of the Incas was Pachacuti (1438-71). He was followed by Topa Inca (1471-93) and Huayna Capac (1493-1525). At the end of the reign of Huayna Capac, the Incas controlled an area 200 miles wide and 2,200 miles long. This vast empire was unified into a single state with a centralized administration.

Roads

A complex network of roads linked all of the empire. The longest was the Andean road, which ran through the mountains (below). Distances were marked out at regular intervals, while rivers and ravines were crossed using suspension bridges (main picture). Runners carried messages, and kept Cuzco informed of events in different regions.

Peoples of the Inca empire

For more than 10,000 years, different peoples have inhabited the region that stretches from the Andean valleys to the Pacific (left). Since its foundation, the Inca empire defeated and absorbed those still around, including the Chanca, the Colla, and the powerful Chimú kingdom.

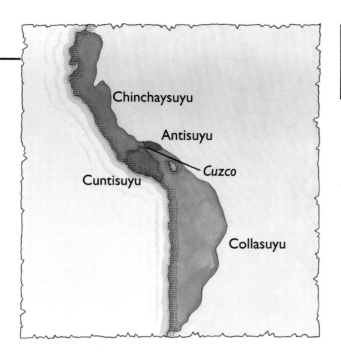

Chinchaysuyu

Antisuyu

Cuzco

Cuntisuyu

Collasuyu

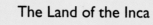

The Land of the Inca

The territories eventually covered by the Inca empire, included all types of climate and landscape. The coastal region is a narrow strip of desert where rain seldom falls (left). From here, the Andes rise steeply to a high plateau that is broken by deep valley basins which offer excellent, arable land. To the east of the mountains lies the vast jungle of the Amazon river basin.

The four quarters

By 1525 the empire stretched from Ecuador to Chile. Tahuantinsuyu, or "Land of the Four Quarters," as it was known, was split into Chinchaysuyu (northwest), Antisuyu (northeast), Cuntinsuyu (southwest) and Collasuyu (southeast) (above), with Cuzco, meaning "navel," at its center.

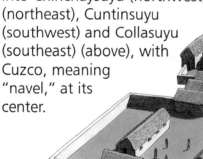

The emperor

The Sapa Inca ("Supreme Inca") ruled by divine right. Worshiped as the "Son of the Sun," his life was governed by elaborate ritual. Each Inca ruler built his own palace (left) in the center of Cuzco. The interior was richly decorated. Its walls were adorned with gold and silver, and hung with textiles. When he died, the emperor's body was preserved and kept in his own palace, while his successor built another.

The Nazca lines

The landscape of the Inca empire was filled with the relics of the people who had previously inhabited the continent. Perhaps the most mysterious are the famous Nazca "lines," which form vast figures in the desert. These were made by scraping away the top surface of stones off the desert floor to expose the lighter soil that lay beneath.

These designs include triangles, rectangles,

spirals, and even animal or bird forms. Scholars think the lines had astronomical significance, or were linked to cults connected with the sea, sky, and mountains.

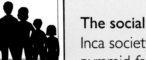

THE INCA EMPIRE

A highly organized control system was needed to ensure the smooth running of the empire. New territories were ruled by Inca-trained officials from newly built towns. Populations in conquered regions were required to comply with Inca laws and with Sun worship. The basic unit of the social structure was the *ayllu*, a farming community based on the family. Throughout the empire each individual, from the top of the social hierarchy to the bottom, had a clearly defined role. Law-abiding subjects were looked after by the state, but harsh penalties were given to those who failed in their duties.

The social hierarchy

Inca society was organized in a pyramid-fashion (below). At its head was the Sapa Inca, whose power was absolute. His principal wife, according to a custom initiated by Pachacuti, was his sister. She was known as the Coya (empress). The Sapa Inca was supported by a supreme council made up of four viceroys, each responsible for one quarter of the kingdom. Below these came the provincial governors, who enjoyed various privileges and could wear special clothing. Curacas, the former chiefs of conquered regions, formed a secondary elite and served as administrators. At the bottom were the commoners.

Building for earthquakes

The west coast of North, Central and South America is constantly threatened by earthquakes (left). These are due to sudden movements of the massive plates that make up the earth's crust as they move against each other.

Cuzco and other Inca cities were built to resist earthquakes. Such was the skill of the Inca stonemasons, that walls could be shaken by powerful earth tremors without being damaged.

Clothing

Clothing indicated the social status and where the wearer came from. Garments were usually simple, but those of the elite exhibited a range of colors and patterning that was denied to common people. Male dress was a loincloth, a sleeveless tunic and a cloak. Women wore a sleeveless dress secured by a waist-sash, and a cape fastened by a pin (left). Male symbols of status included metal breast ornaments and bracelets. The Sapa Inca wore a braid, wound around the head, called a *llauta*.

Town planning

The Inca art of town planning (right) may have been learned from the Chimú. Around Cuzco's central plaza, called "the Holy Place," were the palaces of the Sapa Inca and his predecessors. The Sun Temple was nearby. The rest of the city was divided into four, like the empire. Visitors to Cuzco were required to stay in the quarter that corresponded to their province.

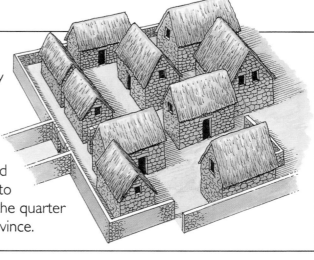

Conquered territories

When a new province was conquered by the Inca army (below), its resources were assessed and recorded on quipus. While one part of all fertile land was assigned to the Sun, a second share went to the emperor. What was left was divided among the ayllus. The *curacas*, the former chiefs, carried out Inca customs and laws.

Quipu

To administer their vast empire, the Incas relied on the *quipu*. This ingenious device consisted of cords of various thicknesses and colors. This allowed the Incas to keep accounts and records. Numbers and other data were indicated by knots of different sizes and positions on the strings. Quipus were tied and "read" by specially appointed officials named *quipucamayocs* (quipu keepers – main picture). With these, the Incas were able to keep records of population, goods, herds, and weapons throughout the empire. Sadly, with the collapse of the Inca empire, the ability to read the quipu died out, and today their language remains a mystery.

INCA RELIGION

Religion cemented the unity of the Inca empire. At its heart was the cult of Inti, the Sun. Other important deities were Mamaquilla (the Moon), Pachamama (Mother Earth), Mamacocha (Mother Water) and Illapa (Thunder). These gods all represented Viracocha, the Creator. The Incas also worshipped holy sites, called *huacas*. The High Priest of the Sun and his assistants belonged to the imperial family. Mamacunas (chosen women) lived in convents. It was their duty to teach the *acllas* (virgins).

The Inca Calendar
The Incas observed the sun, moon and stars. They established a solar calendar of twelve months, in accordance with the sun's position in the sky, which was marked by special stones (below). The Inca calendar cycle was respected throughout the empire.

The Sapa Inca
To assert his power, each ruler claimed to be the son of the Sun. As the Sun ruled the skies, so the Supreme Inca ruled on Earth. When the Sapa Inca died, it was said that the Sun had summoned him. The bodies of dead rulers were mummified and were consulted as oracles (right). Their wishes were interpreted by the living Sapa Inca.

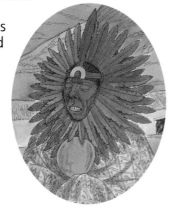

Ceremony and Sacrifice
Religion was the focus for the entire Inca empire. One third of everything was passed on to the cult of Inti and the priests (right), who held an important position in Inca society. Llamas and guinea pigs formed part of this "taxation." If these were free from blemishes they were sacrificed to the air, frost and water in order to ensure a good harvest. Sacrifices were also made to the Sun as it rose every day over the city of Cuzco.

The cult of the Sun

Inti, the Sun, was worshipped as the "giver of life." Temples for the cult of Inti were built throughout the empire. At Cuzco's main temple the Incas kept gold images of the Sun (main picture). Herds and produce belonging to the Sun were used in rituals and as offerings. The cult's festivals were closely tied to the growing of crops (above). Inti Raimi, the Feast of the Sun, was celebrated on the winter solstice in the month belonging to June.

Egyptian sun worship

From very early times the sun was also worshipped in the Nile Valley. During the Old and Middle Kingdoms of Egypt (c.2666-1640 B.C.), the supreme deity was Ra, the Sun God (below). His symbols were the pyramid and the obelisk, and he was shown sailing the heavens in a boat. The cult of Ra showed itself most clearly in the raising of magnificent temples. For Egyptians, Ra was embodied in the Pharaohs, who were worshiped in the same way as Ra himself.

Mummification

The Incas revered the remains of their ancestors. After the death of each emperor, his internal organs were removed and buried, and his body preserved. Dressed in fine fabrics and surrounded by precious objects, the bodies remained in the palace that each had inhabited in life. Thousands of years before, the Egyptians had also mummified their dead, and in South America, the Paracas people placed mummy bundles in deep caves (right).

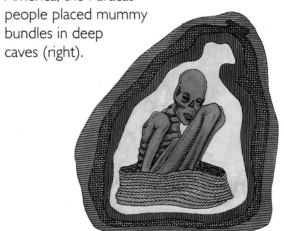

INCA SOCIETY

Most commoners lived in farming and pastoral communities. Land and herds were divided into three parts. The first part belonged to the cult of the Sun. The second belonged to the Sapa Inca, his family and servants. The third was shared by members of the ayllu. Taxes, or tribute payments, were calculated in terms of work. Inspectors controlled all aspects of life within the empire. The material needs of each family were assured by the empire. In return for total obedience, the Inca state guaranteed lifelong security.

Housing

Other cultures, like the Chanca and the Colla favored round houses, but Inca dwellings were rectangular (below). Often built from stone with thatched roofs, they were virtually unfurnished and contained few possessions. All homes were visited by inspectors, who checked living standards.

Terraces

The steep slopes of the Andes were covered in fertile, well-watered terraces, built by the Incas (main picture).

Farming

Farmers used hoes, digging sticks, and foot-ploughs with a point of hard wood or bronze. Throughout the empire, two systems of agriculture flourished. At high altitudes, people tended herds of llama and alpaca, and cultivated *quinoa* (a nourishing cereal) and over 200 varieties of potato. Maize was grown in warm valleys and on low-lying, well-irrigated slopes (right). Hotter lowland products included cotton, avocado pears, tomatoes, squashes, chilli peppers, beans, peanuts, honey, and fruits.

Animals

Crucial to the Andean way of life were the llama, alpaca, vicuña, and guanaco, known collectively as *cameloids*. In the highland pastures of Peru and Bolivia, herds of domesticated llama and alpaca were kept as pack animals and for wool (right). The guanaco and vicuña roamed freely. The guinea pig was kept by most households, and used as a regular source of meat.

Taxation

Taxation took the form of forced labor, or *mit'a*. For set periods, men provided labor for road building, mining and the construction of fortresses, and terraces. Women wove cloth, while children and elderly people did light work. Each province provided amounts of tribute in food and goods for the state's storehouses (below), that were used in times of hardship.

Terracing is still used in many parts of the world, such as Indonesia (below), where steep hillsides make normal agriculture impossible. It increases the area of land available, and prevents erosion of the soil.

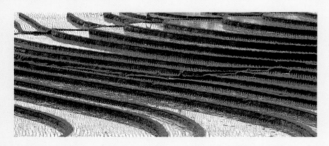

Reed boats

The Incas were largely a land-based people. Coastal populations, and those living on lakes, used bundles of dried reeds to construct lightweight boats (below). Some were small one-person vessels, but others had space for numerous passengers. Today, on Lake Titicaca (in Peru), similar reed boats are still used for catching fish..

ARTS AND SCIENCES

Luxury goods were produced by specialists, whose calling was usually hereditary. These specialists lived in cities, and did not have to pay tribute. They included metalsmiths, jewelers, and experts in weaving. The Incas also excelled as stonemasons. Inca architecture was characterised by its simplicity and solidity. Huge granite blocks fitted together so closely that no mortar was needed. Even today, a knife cannot be inserted between them.

Jewelry
Inca jewelers were exceptionally skilled in the creation of ornaments from a variety of gemstones and rare materials (top). Jewelry often indicated the social rank of a person. The Spanish referred to the Inca elite as *orejones*, or "big ears," because of the large earspools they wore (below).

Music
Music was played at the Inca court and during important ceremonies. Wind instruments included a cane flute called a *quena*, and panpipes

made by tying together different lengths of cane (left). In war, conch shell trumpets and bone flutes were used. Drums came in various sizes. Some were made from the skins of enemy warriors.

Textiles
Women in each household spun and wove to provide cloth for their families, as they do today (above). Luxury cloth was produced by specialist male weavers. These luxury textiles were decorated with gold and silver ornaments.

Arts and crafts

Professional artisans worked full-time for the emperor, members of the elite, and the temple. Fine pottery vessels were made in a variety of shapes by Inca potters. Gold and silver were reserved for luxury and ceremonial objects. Both the Chimú and the Incas were skilled metalsmiths. Gold was the symbolic color of the Sun and the Sapa Inca, while silver represented the moon and the Coya. In the emperor's palace gardens, plants and animals were reproduced in gold and silver.

Chimú hand of gold

Inca pottery vessel

Machu Picchu

Machu Picchu is the best preserved of all Inca towns (main picture). After the Spanish conquest, it lay forgotten until its rediscovery in 1911 by Hiram Bingham, the North American explorer. Situated high in the Andes, Machu Picchu is a natural fortress protected by steep slopes. Flanking the central plaza are public buildings, the palace and the Sun Temple. Hillsides were terraced for growing crops.

Animal breeding

By 2000 B.C., Andean peoples had domesticated the llama (below). These animals were bred for the quality of their wool, and for use as pack animals. Guinea pigs were bred for their meat. Sick animals were killed and buried, to prevent the spread of disease.

Weaving

Weavers used cotton and wool from domesticated llama or alpaca herds and from wild vicuña or guanaco. As in ancient Mexico, textiles were produced on the backstrap loom (left). This method, still used today, requires the warp threads to be stretched between two bars, one of which is tied to a post. The width of the cloth is limited by the weaver's armspan.

THE SPANISH CONQUEST

In 1532, when Spanish forces reached the coast of Peru, Atahuallpa, and Huascar, the sons of Huayna Capac, were quarrelling over succession. Francisco Pizarro was able to conquer the divided Inca empire with just 63 horsemen and 200 foot soldiers. Most of the Inca empire became the Viceroyalty of Peru and remained so until 1824, despite various Amerindian uprisings. In Mexico, Hernán Cortés began his conquest in 1519. By 1521, the capital of the Aztecs had been reduced to rubble and their empire destroyed. Renamed "New Spain," the land remained a colony until 1821. Today the populations of Peru and Mexico are largely of mixed European and Amerindian descent.

El Dorado
"El Dorado" means "the Golden Man," and was the name given to a legendary chief who anointed himself with gold-dust. Popular imagination transformed El Dorado into a city of gold and many other sites, including a volcanic lake (below).

Disease
The native inhabitants of the Americas proved vulnerable to diseases from Europe. Weakened by overwork in mines and on plantations, countless Amerindians died from epidemics such as smallpox. The spread of these diseases was far more devastating than the bubonic plague that ravaged Europe in the 1300s (below).

Cortés
Hernán Cortés (1485-1547 – below) landed in Mexico with approximately 600 men, armed with metal weapons, gunpowder and horses. They were assisted in their conquest by the Tlaxcalans and other peoples, eager to free themselves from Aztec oppression. Moctezuma II allowed the Spaniards into his capital. He was taken prisoner, and the Aztec army was defeated.

Felipe Guamán Poma de Ayala

A unique record of 16th-century Inca life survives. Its author, Felipe Guamán Poma de Ayala, was a native Andean. He was angered and saddened by the sufferings of his people, and decided to petition the Spanish King. The resulting manuscript of 1,188 pages, includes 398 drawings (right). His work explores all aspects of Inca history and religion, and describes events and customs throughout the destroyed empire.

Torture and brutality

The native South Americans were no match for Spaniards, armed with gunpowder and steel weapons (main picture). Once in control, Spanish rule was marked by many acts of cruelty. In the Mexican province of Michoacán, Nuño de Guzmán burned villages and murdered chiefs. The Tarascan king was dragged behind a horse, then burned alive. Amerindians were worked to exhaustion in mines, by Spanish settlers.

The Catholic Church

The Spanish conquerors came in search of gold, but they also sought to implant Christianity and win souls. In their desire to banish pagan beliefs, they destroyed idols and burned codices. Using stones from pyramids and temples, they built churches and cathedrals (below). A few clerics did, however, keep a detailed record of everything they saw and heard.

Pizarro

Francisco Pizarro (c.1475-1541 – below) started the conquest of Peru in 1532. The Inca empire was weakened by civil war. Like Cortés, Pizarro took advantage of the divided loyalties of conquered people. Atahuallpa, treacherously taken prisoner by Pizarro, sought to regain his freedom by filling his prison with gold. After a mock trial, however, the Inca was put to death in 1533. Pizarro was later killed by fellow Spaniards during a leadership feud.

THE MODERN WORLD

In Peru, the ancient language Quechua is still used by millions of highland Amerindians who have inherited various traits from their Inca ancestors. In Mexico, the descendants of the Aztecs, now called the Nahua, number over 1.4 million people. Most speak Spanish, but some speak only Nahuatl. Although the Nahua no longer build pyramids or paint codices, they still weave textiles, and celebrate traditional festivals, such as the Festival of the Dead. Celebrated in Mexico, it falls on the Christian feasts of All Saints and All Souls, highlighting the fusion between the pre- and post-Conquest worlds.

Diego Rivera
The brightly colored codices and paintings of the ancient Mexicans were inspiration for the Mexican artist, Diego Rivera (1886-1957). On the walls of buildings, he painted scenes from Aztec life, showing it in all its splendor (below).

Food and drugs
Old World cuisines were enriched by the introduction of New World foods such as potatoes, tomatoes, avocados, peanuts, vanilla, and turkeys. Xocoatl (pronounced "chocoatl") was the Nahuatl word for chocolate. Now cocoa beans are widely grown in Africa and other parts of the world. So too is maize (right), once central to Aztec and Inca survival. Tobacco, a native of the Americas, was introduced to Europe in the 16th century. The Andeans have traditionally chewed coca leaves to numb the effects of cold and hunger. Today coca makes huge fortunes for cocaine dealers.

Archaeology

As time passes, archaeologists are able to tell us more about the civilizations of the Americas. In Cuzco, the monastery of Santo Domingo stands on the walls of the Coricancha, or Sun Temple, and over recent years, the original Inca structure has been partially uncovered. In the heart of Mexico City, excavations are revealing the sacred precinct of the Aztecs (right).

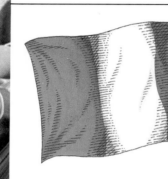

Peru

Modern Peru has approximately 21 million people. Nearly half are Amerindians, descendants of the country's original inhabitants (main picture). Although Cuzco was rebuilt soon after the Conquest by Spanish settlers, it still attracts many tourists who are drawn by the ruins of Inca civilization that have survived.

Mexico

Approximately 300 years after the collapse of the Aztec empire, the descendants of Spanish settlers and native people won independence from Spain. In memory of the Aztecs (Mexica), the country was renamed Mexico. Today the population of Mexico exceeds 90 million. Although Spanish is the official language, 56 Amerindian languages are spoken by over 7 million people.

Mexico City

Mexico City (right), with approximately 20 million inhabitants, is one of the largest cities in the world. Built on the ruins of Aztec Tenochtitlan, it offers the same amenities as cities in the United States or Europe. A complex drainage system prevents the city's foundations from sinking into the subsoil of the ancient lake-bed. Steel and reinforced concrete enable architects and engineers to build tall, earthquake-resistant buildings.

Incas:

c.1100 Cuzco founded by the legendary Manco Capac, first Sapa Inca

1450 Pachacuti, the 9th Sapa Inca, enlarges the Inca empire by a series of local wars

1498 Huayna Capac, the 11th Sapa Inca, extends conquest into Colombia

1527 Francisco Pizarro makes first landing. Death of Huayna Capac is followed by civil war

1532 Francisco Pizarro captures the Inca emperor Atahuallpa

1533 Atahuallpa is executed by the Spanish

1535 Collapse of the Inca empire

Aztecs:

1325 The Aztecs settle at Tenochtitlan

1440-68 Reign of Moctezuma I, father of the Aztec empire

1486-1502 Extension of the empire

1502-20 Reign of Moctezuma II and consolidation of the empire

1519 Arrival of Hernán Cortés and his soldiers

1521 Tenochtitlan destroyed by Spanish soldiers after a long siege

1525 Collapse of the Aztec empire

8000 B.C.

First hieroglyphs (picture writing) in Egypt c.3500 B.C.

Old Kingdom in Egypt 2628-2181 B.C.

Pyramids built in Egypt during Old Kingdom

Egyptian Middle Kingdom 2181-1567 B.C.

2000 B.C.

Tutankhamun – the boy pharoah 1361-1237 B.C.

New Kingdom in Egypt 1567-1085 B.C.

Romulus and Remus found the city of Rome 753 B.C.

500 B.C.

Roman Empire c.27 B.C.-c.A.D. 476

Julius Caesar murdered 44 B.C.

Fall of the Roman Empire A.D. 476

Viking raids on Britain and France A.D. 793-1000

A.D. 1000 First Crusade to recapture Holy Land from Muslims A.D. 1096

First mechanical clock developed

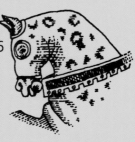

The Aztec Empire in Central America A.D. 1300-1521

A.D. 1350-1532 Growth of the Inca Empire in South America

8000-5650 B.C.
First cities – Jericho and Catal Hüyük

3500-3000 B.C.
Wheel invented by the Sumerians

Early Minoan period in Crete begins c.2500 B.C.

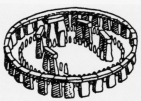

Stonehenge completed in England c.1500 B.C.

The destruction of Knossos in Crete. End of the Minoan period c.1200 B.C.

c.500 B.C. Life of Gautama the Buddha

c.1400-1027 B.C. Shang dynasty in China

Birth of Confucius 551 B.C.

The Golden Age of Greece 478-405 B.C.

Alexander the Great conquers Persia, Syria and Egypt 331 B.C.

The first Empire in China 221 B.C.-A.D. 618

The Great Wall in China completed in 214 B.C.

Samurai warriors of Japan from A.D. 1100-1850

The Plague, or Black Death, spreads throughout Europe A.D. 1347.

First mechanical printing press developed by Gutenberg in Germany in A.D. 1455.

Christopher Columbus sets sail for the West Indies and became the first European to discover America.

GLOSSARY

Acllas Young girls who lived in convents and were taught religious duties by the Mamacunas. Some Acllas became Virgins of the Sun.

Adobe Unfired mud-brick, dried in the sun.

Ayllu Traditional family or community group.

Cameloid Belonging to the Camelidae family: includes the domestic llama and alpaca; also the wild guanaco and vicuña.

Codex Mexican codices were pictorial manuscripts painted on deerskin, bark paper, or agave paper.

Curaca Ex-chief from subdued regions of the Inca empire.

Huaca Places or objects regarded as holy by the Incas and their subjects.

Mamacunas Consecrated or Chosen Women who lived in convents and served the Inca religion.

Mestizo Person of mixed European and Indian descent.

Mit'a Public-works tax paid by Inca subjects.

Nahuatl The language of the Aztecs; in contemporary Mexico it is spoken by around 1.4 million people.

Quechua Language spoken by the Incas and by Andean peoples related to the Incas.

Quetzal Bird with long green tail feathers, from the cloudy mountains of Guatemala and the Mexican state of Chiapas.

Quipu Knotted cords used by the Incas for recording information.

Tahuantinsuyu Inca empire: "Land of the four Quarters." At its center was Cuzco.

INDEX

Photographic credits:
Abbreviations: t-top, m-middle, b-bottom,
r-right, l-left
Cover, 3t, 12, 15t, 22t, 28t & b: Roger Vlitos;
2t, 3m & b, 4b, 20t, 23, 24t, ml, bl &br, 28m;
Frank Spooner Pictures; 2m, 5, 17, 20b, 22b,
24mr, 25, 29b: Trip; 2b, 21b, 26t, 27tl & tr:
South American Pictures; 4t, 15b, 16, 21t: Eye
Ubiquitous; 7, 8, 14, 27b, 28-29, 29t:
Mexicolore; 11t, 26b; Mary Evans Picture
Library; 11m & b; Jenny Gosnold; 27m: Solution
Pictures.